A Robbie Reader

What's So
Great About . . .?
MICHELLE
OBAMA

Joanne Mattern

Mitchell Lane
PUBLISHERS

P.O. Box 196
Hockessin, Delaware 19707
Visit us on the web: www.mitchelllane.com
Comments? email us: mitchelllane@mitchelllane.com

Mitchell Lane
PUBLISHERS

Printing   1   2   3   4   5   6   7   8   9

A Robbie Reader
What's So Great About . . . ?

Amelia Earhart	Anne Frank	Annie Oakley
Barack Obama	The Buffalo Soldiers	Christopher Columbus
Daniel Boone	Davy Crockett	The Donner Party
Elizabeth Blackwell	Ferdinand Magellan	Francis Scott Key
Galileo	George Washington Carver	Harriet Tubman
Helen Keller	Henry Hudson	Jacques Cartier
Johnny Appleseed	King Tut	Lewis and Clark
Martin Luther King Jr.	Michelle Obama	Paul Bunyan
Pocahontas	Robert Fulton	Rosa Parks
Sam Houston	The Tuskegee Airmen	

Library of Congress Cataloging-in-Publication Data
Mattern, Joanne, 1963–
  What's so great about Michelle Obama / by Joanne Mattern.
    p. cm. — (A Robbie reader) (What's so great about . . . ?)
  Includes bibliographical references and index.
  ISBN 978-1-58415-833-2 (library bound)
1. Obama, Michelle, 1964– —Juvenile literature. 2. Presidents' spouses—United States—Biography—Juvenile literature. 3. Legislators' spouses—United States—Biography—Juvenile literature. 4. African American women lawyers—Illinois—Chicago—Biography—Juvenile literature. 5. Chicago (Ill.)—Biography—Juvenile literature I. Title.
  E909.O24M376 2010
  973.932092—dc22
  [B]

                                                                  2009027357

ABOUT THE AUTHOR: Joanne Mattern is the author of more than 250 books for children. She has written biographies about many famous people for Mitchell Lane Publishers, including *Peyton Manning, Ashley Tisdale, The Jonas Brothers, LeBron James,* and *Drake Bell and Josh Peck.* Joanne also enjoys writing about animals, reading, and being outdoors. She lives in New York State with her husband, four children, and several pets.

PUBLISHER'S NOTE: The following story has been thoroughly researched and to the best of our knowledge represents a true story. Documentation of such research appears on page 29. While every possible effort has been made to ensure accuracy, the publisher will not assume liability for damages caused by inaccuracies in the data, and makes no warranty on the accuracy of the information contained herein.

TABLE OF CONTENTS

Words in **bold** type can be found in the glossary.

her children, Malia and Sasha. "I come here as a mom whose girls are the heart of my heart and the center of my world," she told the crowd.

Michelle talked about why it was so important to make the United States a strong nation. The number one reason was her children, and all the children in the world. She said, "Their future—and all our children's future—is my stake in this election."

Michelle's speech on the first night of the Democratic National Convention was one of the highlights of the event. She proved that she could hold her own on a national stage.

Barack and Michelle Obama read to a second-grade class at the Capital City Public Charter School in Washington, D.C. They have made community service an important part of their roles as President and First Lady.

Michelle Obama's speech was a huge success. A few months later, Barack Obama became the 44th president of the United States. His wife, Michelle, would be a First Lady like no other.

Left to right: brother Craig, father Fraser Robinson, baby Michelle, and mother Marian Robinson. Michelle comes from a close-knit family.

CHAPTER TWO

Growing Up

Michelle LaVaughn Robinson was born in Chicago, Illinois, on January 17, 1964. Her parents were Marian and Fraser Robinson. Fraser Robinson worked for Chicago's water department. Marian stayed home to raise her children. Michelle had a brother, Craig, who was two years older than she.

Fraser Robinson was a hard worker. However, when Michelle was a little girl, he became sick with a disease called multiple sclerosis (MUL-tih-pul sklur-OH-sis), or MS. Multiple sclerosis affects the muscles. People who have MS often have trouble walking and moving. The disease forced Fraser Robinson to walk with a limp. Later, he would need a cane to help him walk. In 1991, he would die of causes related to MS.

Mr. Robinson continued to work, even when he was sick. Michelle and Craig learned a lot from their father's example. "He was a man with a **disability** . . . but he got up and went to work every day," Michelle said in a speech many years later. "He was a man who didn't complain, was never late, never expressed any level of doubt about his situation in life, and taught us that we could dream of anything."

Marian and Fraser Robinson expected Michelle and Craig to do their best. The hours after school were filled with homework and studying. School was easy for Craig, but Michelle had a harder time. She had to spend extra time studying to earn top grades.

Michelle graduated from a neighborhood elementary school in 1977. Then she attended Whitney M. Young Magnet High School. This school had students from all over the city.

Michelle graduated from Whitney Young in 1981. At that time, Craig was going to Princeton. Princeton is an **elite** college in New Jersey. Craig had no trouble getting into

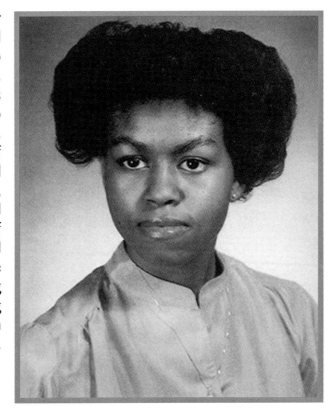

Michelle in her high school graduation photo from 1981. Education was very important to Michelle's family. Instead of attending a local high school, Michelle traveled to another part of Chicago to attend the more demanding Whitney Young Magnet High School.

Princeton because he had good grades and was a top **athlete**. Michelle was determined to go to Princeton, too. "I knew him, and I knew his study habits," she said, "and I was like, 'I can do that too.' "

Michelle was right. Princeton accepted her. In September 1981, Michelle headed east to find a whole new world.

Michelle graduated from Princeton University in 1985. She found herself in the minority among the mostly white students at Princeton. Attending this school helped Michelle understand her own identity and what her role could be in the black community.

Fitting In

Michelle had grown up in a neighborhood that was mostly African American. Later, she had attended a high school that had students from many different **racial** and **ethnic** backgrounds. However, almost all the students at Princeton were white. For the first time in her life, Michelle was a **minority**.

When Michelle was a senior, she wrote a long paper, or **thesis**, called "Princeton-Educated Blacks and the Black Community." She sent questions to hundreds of black students and graduates of Princeton. She wondered how Princeton shaped their feelings. She asked whether black students would be more or less likely to help the black community after attending a mostly white school. Michelle hoped her research would help her see what her own role in society might be.

In her thesis, Michelle wrote, "My experiences at Princeton have made me far more aware of my 'blackness' than ever before." She felt that others saw her as "black first and a student second."

Michelle and her brother believed that their parents had given them **confidence** to succeed in a world that might not value them. Craig Robinson told a newspaper, "When you grow up as a black kid in a white world, so many times people are telling you . . . you're not good enough. To have a family who constantly reminded you how smart you were, how good you were, how pleasant it was to be around you, how successful you could be, it's hard to combat. Our parents gave us a little head start by making us feel confident."

Michelle's confidence helped her do very well at Princeton. She graduated with honors in 1985. Then she studied to be a lawyer at Harvard Law School.

Michelle and her brother, Craig, have been close throughout their lives.

Michelle worked hard at Harvard and did well. She also worked to help the community. She worked with a group that gave legal help to poor people in the neighborhood. Helping others was something that would be important to Michelle all her life.

Michelle graduated from Harvard Law in 1988. She took a job as a lawyer at Sidley Austin. Michelle would learn a lot there. Best of all, she would be going home to Chicago.

Michelle and Barack Obama married on October 3, 1992, after working together at the law firm Sidley Austin.

CHAPTER
FOUR

Life with Barack

In 1989, Michelle's boss at Sidley Austin asked her to help a law student who was going to work at the company for a few months. The student's name was Barack Obama.

Michelle and Barack had a lot in common. Both of them had gone to Harvard Law. Both valued education and family. Both wanted to help people who were less fortunate.

Michelle and Barack became good friends. In October 1992, Barack and Michelle got married.

In 1991, Michelle went to work for Chicago's mayor, Richard Daley. Michelle's job was to help businesses in Chicago. In 1993, she became the Executive Director of Public Allies. Public Allies trained young people to work in the area of **public service**. Michelle loved her job. At the time, she called it "by far the best thing I've done in my professional career."

In 1996, Barack was elected to be an Illinois state senator. He spent most of his time 200 miles away from home in Springfield, the state capital.

Michelle and Barack also wanted to start a family. Michelle knew she needed a less demanding job if she wanted to be a mother. She left Public Allies and started working part time at the University of Chicago. The university was near the Obamas' home. Michelle worked to involve students in the social issues of the neighborhood and the city.

In July 1998, Michelle gave birth to her first daughter, Malia Ann. The couple's second daughter, Natasha (who is called Sasha), was born in 2001.

In 2004, Barack was elected a United States Senator. Now he would work in Washington, D.C., while Michelle stayed home

The Obama family celebrates Barack's U.S. Senate win in November 2004. They have always kept their children as the focus of their lives, even when Barack began getting national attention.

in Chicago. By then, Michelle was working for the University of Chicago Medical Center.

Barack was becoming very famous and popular. In November 2004, he gave an important speech at the Democratic National Convention. His speech was so exciting that everyone in the country talked about it. Soon afterward, he started to think about running for president.

When Barack was elected president in 2008, the Obamas became the first African American family to live in the White House. Michelle soon showed she was a stylish and energetic First Lady.

CHAPTER FIVE

First Lady

Michelle left her job. She made running for president a family affair. "The way I look at it is, we're running for president of the United States. Me, Barack, Sasha, Malia, my mom, my brother, his sisters—we're all running," she said.

Michelle became a powerful ally in her husband's run for president. She gave speeches all over the country and appeared on television. Many people liked Michelle. They believed in her message. Just like many Americans, Michelle wanted the best future for her children. She wanted people to overcome **obstacles** in their lives. Michelle understood that many Americans were struggling. She recalled how her parents had worked to give her and Craig a good life, even though her

2009

Sometimes being part of the First Family is a glamorous job. Barack and Michelle set the style as they appear at the Inaugural (in-AW-gyur-ul) Ball in January 2009.

Barack's inauguration was a historic moment for America. Michelle was proud to hold the Bible as her husband swore the oath of office before a huge crowd in Washington, D.C. Their daughters, Malia and Sasha, looked on.

father was disabled. Michelle helped spread Barack's message of hope to all Americans.

On November 4, 2008, Americans elected Barack Obama as their president. For the first time, an African American family would live in the White House. Michelle's mother also moved into the White House to help the family settle into their new lives.

Michelle and Barack found that living in the White House was great for their children. For the first time, Barack was home for breakfast and dinner almost every day. "We have dinner as a family together every night, and Barack, when he's not traveling, tucks the girls in," Michelle told *People* magazine. "We haven't had that time together for years."

Once she was sure her family was happy, Michelle began to figure out her role as First Lady. One of her goals was to encourage people to volunteer in their communities. In June 2009, she launched a project called United We Serve. Michelle called the project "a nationwide effort calling on all Americans to make service a part of their daily lives."

IRAQ AND AFGHANISTAN

Michelle, Malia, Sasha, and Michelle's brother, Craig, help pack care packages for service personnel stationed in Iraq and Afghanistan. The Obamas have always placed great importance on community service.

First Lady Michelle Obama rallies support for the Capital Area Food Bank, which provides food for the less fortunate. Jill Biden, wife of Vice President Joe Biden, stands at Michelle's left.

Michelle takes a hands-on approach to her United We Serve organization by joining a local Habitat for Humanity building project.

Michelle hands out meals to the homeless—and poses for a photo—at Miriam's Kitchen in Washington, D.C. She has always enjoyed volunteering and helping others in the community.

Michelle also spends a lot of time helping her country. She especially enjoys meeting with community groups and telling Barack what she learns. Michelle's goal is to help her husband understand what people need to make their lives better.

"I think people are ready for something different," Michelle said a few months before the election. "I'm ready for the highs, and I'm ready for the lows. But I'm also ready to work with my husband in the White House and lead this country to a different place."

CHRONOLOGY

1964   Michelle LaVaughn Robinson is born on January 17.

1977   She graduates from elementary school.

1981   She graduates from Whitney M. Young Magnet High School in Chicago.

1985   Michelle graduates from Princeton University.

1988   She graduates from Harvard Law School and accepts a job as a lawyer at Sidley Austin.

1989   She meets Barack Obama.

1991   Michelle accepts a job with Chicago mayor Richard Daley.

1992   Michelle marries Barack on October 3.

1993   She accepts job as executive director of Public Allies.

1996   Barack becomes an Illinois state senator.

1998   Their daughter Malia Ann is born; Michelle works part-time at the University of Chicago.

2001   Their daughter Natasha (Sasha) is born; Michelle works at the University of Chicago Medical Center.

2004   Barack is elected to the United States Senate; he gives the keynote speech at the Democratic National Convention.

2007   Barack announces he will run for president of the United States; Michelle leaves her job to campaign with him.

2008   Michelle speaks at the Democratic National Convention in August; Barack is elected president in November.

2009   Barack is inaugurated as president; the Obama family moves into the White House; Michelle begins the United We Serve project to encourage Americans to volunteer.

TIMELINE IN HISTORY

1868   The Fourteenth Amendment secures citizenship rights for all Americans, including African Americans.

1870   The Fifteenth Amendment guarantees voting rights for African American men.

1896   The Supreme Court says separate but equal facilities for blacks and whites are legal.

1909   The National Association for the Advancement of Colored People (NAACP) is organized.

1920s   Millions of African Americans migrate from the South to the North in search of better job opportunities and less discrimination.

1929   The Great Depression begins in the United States.

1954   The Supreme Court says schools in the United States should be desegregated.

1963   Dr. Martin Luther King Jr. gives his "I Have a Dream" speech at the March on Washington for Jobs and Freedom in Washington, D.C.

1964   President Lyndon B. Johnson signs the Civil Rights Act of 1964.

1967   Thurgood Marshall becomes the first African American Supreme Court Justice.

1968   Civil rights activist Martin Luther King Jr. is assassinated in Memphis.

1981   Sandra Day O'Connor becomes the first female Supreme Court Justice.

2000   President William Jefferson Clinton signs the National Underground Railroad Freedom Center Act.

2006   Ceremonial groundbreaking takes place on the National Mall for the Dr. Martin Luther King, Jr., Memorial.

2009   Members of the Obama family become the first African American residents of the White House.

FIND OUT MORE

Books

Bodden, Valerie. *Michelle Obama: First Lady and Role Model.* Edina, Minnesota: ABDO, 2010.

Brill, Marlene Targ. *Michelle Obama: From Chicago's South Side to the White House.* Minneapolis: Lerner Publishing, 2009.

Brophy, David Bergen. *Michelle Obama: Meet the First Lady.* New York: Scholastic, 2009.

Colbert, David. *Michelle Obama: An American Story.* Boston: Houghton Mifflin, 2009.

Edwards, Roberta. *Michelle Obama: Mom-in-Chief.* New York: Grosset & Dunlap, 2009.

Gormley, Beatrice. *Barack Obama: Our 44th President.* New York: Aladdin, 2008.

Hudson, Amanda. *Michelle Obama.* Pleasantville, New York: Gareth Stevens Publishing, 2010.

Works Consulted

Barack Obama and Joe Biden
    http://www.barackobama.com/about/michelle_obama

First Lady Michelle Obama
    http://www.whitehouse.gov/administration/michelle_obama

Kenigsburg, Elizabeth. "Michelle Obama Defines Own Role as First Lady." America.gov, June 29, 2009.
    http://www.america.gov/st/usg-english/2009/June/20090629092010degrebsginek0,475445.html

Leiby, Richard. "First Lady's Job? Slowly, It's Hers to Define." *Washington Post,* February 19, 2009.
    http://www.washingtonpost.com/wp-dyn/content/article/2009/02/19/AR2009021903435.html

FIND OUT MORE

Lisi, Clemente. "A Peek Inside Michelle Obama's White House." *The New York Post,* February 25, 2009. http://www.nypost.com/p/news/national/peek_inside_Michelle_Obama_white_01FEKGBVIkwqVF2vqwEb9N

"Michelle Obama Finds White House Life Good for Kids." *People,* May 21, 2009. http://www.people.com/people/article/0,20280290,00.html

Mundy, Liza. *Michelle: A Biography.* New York: Simon & Schuster, 2008.

Obama, Barack. *The Audacity of Hope.* New York: Crown, 2006.

Obama, Michelle. *Michelle Obama: In Her Own Words—The Speeches, 2008.* CreateSpace, 2008.

Wolffe, Richard. "Who Is Michelle Obama?" *Newsweek,* February 25, 2008. http://www.newsweek.com/id/112849

On the Internet

Barack Obama Timeline
http://www.enchantedlearning.com/history/us/pres/obama/timeline.shtml

Kids for Obama
http://kids.barackobama.com

President Barack Obama
http://www.enchantedlearning.coom/history/us/pres/obama/index.shtml

United We Serve
http://www.serve.gov

Photo Credits: Cover, pp. 25, 28–29, 30–31, 32–WhiteHouse.gov; p. 1–Richard Termine; p. 3–Chip Somodevilla/Getty Images; p. 4–John Moore/Getty Images; p. 5–Max Whittaker/Getty Images; pp. 6, 26–Pablo Martinez Monsivais/AP Photo; pp. 8, 11, 12–Robinson family. p. 22–AP Photo; p. 24–Getty Images; p. 25–Paul Morigi/Getty Images; p. 25 (bottom)–United We Serve; p. 27–cc-by-sa-2.0. Every effort has been made to locate all copyright holders of material used in this book. If any errors or omissions have occurred, corrections will be made in future editions of the book.

GLOSSARY

athlete (ATH-leet)—Someone who is good at sports.

candidate (KAN-duh-dit)—Someone who is running in an election.

confidence (KON-fuh-dunts)—A strong belief in yourself and your abilities.

convention (kon-VEN-shun)—A political meeting where candidates are chosen.

disability (dis-uh-BIL-uh-tee)—Something that restricts what a person can do.

elite (ee-LEET)—Special, privileged.

ethnic (ETH-nik)—Relating to a large group of people who share a unique background, such as race, religion, language, or culture.

inaugural (in-AW-gyur-ul)—Having to do with taking office, such as the office of president.

minority (my-NAR-ih-tee)—Someone in a group of people whose race or opinions differ from those of most of a population.

nominate (NAH-mih-nayt)—To choose someone for a job.

obstacle (OB-stih-kul)—Something that stands in the way.

priority (pry-OR-uh-tee)—Something that is the most important.

public service (PUB-lik SER-vus)—Working to help other people or the community.

racial (RAY-shul)—Dealing with a person's race (the group of people who share physical traits with the person).

thesis (THEE-sis)—A long paper that proves a point about a topic.